The Story of Hope

A journey from despair to freedom

By Katherine Elizabeth James

Illustrated by Marta Maszkiewicz

Printed in the United Kingdom
First Printing, 2020

ISBN: 978-1-8380130-0-4 (Paperback)
ISBN: 978-1-8380130-1-1 (eBook)

Storyarc Publishing
Hampshire
RG28 7JX

To all those who have
lost hope and found the
courage to start again

Table of Contents

Chapter 1: **Loneliness** 7

Chapter 2: **Despair** 9

Chapter 3: **Doubt** 11

Chapter 4: **Faith** 13

Chapter 5: **Fear** 15

Chapter 6: **Trust** 17

Chapter 7: **Wisdom** 19

Chapter 8: **Confidence** 21

Chapter 9: **Anticipation** 23

Chapter 10: **Courage** 25

Chapter 11: **Perseverance** 27

Chapter 12: **Hope** 29

Chapter 13: **Freedom** 31

Chapter 14: **Redemption** 33

Epilogue 35

Chapter 1: **Loneliness**

Her name is Hope. She lives in an attic room and she is lonely. She has been given a black cloak to wear, made of harsh, worsted material. It drags at her ankles like a heavy leaden weight. It is meant to protect her from the cold, sharp needles of winter, with its bitter chill and driving rain and snow, but it serves no purpose except to drag her down. She longs for a new cloak lined with silk, as light as gossamer. Soft and warm in winter and cool as a balmy breeze in summer, she knows this cloak would help her on her journey.

Today she looks out of the window of her upstairs room. She sees a laughing crowd in party dress. She dreams of joining them but knows she would never fit in. She feels loneliness seep into her bones and fill her warm, loving heart with dark despair.

Chapter 2: **Despair**

Hope is in despair. Born into a world of opportunity, she cannot grasp hold of it and make it her own. She has searched her whole life long for it. It is in the storybooks and fairy tales, which always seem to have a happy ending. She doubts she will ever find it. She so desperately wants it. Despite how sad and empty she feels today, she puts on her cloak to go out and look for it.

Chapter 3: **Doubt**

It is a cold and wintry day. The pavements glisten with freshly fallen snow. The sun peeps through the ice-blue sky to turn Hope's path into a million diamonds. Everything is muffled, save for her measured crunching steps. Although the sun is shining, nothing grows. The days become shorter and Hope feels hemmed in by doubting thoughts. But surely there is some hope out there for her? Her name is Hope. She knows she must believe in herself; then Faith will be her staff and Love will be her guide.

Chapter 4: **Faith**

Hope goes to bed early, looking for inspiration in her dreams. Her linen sheets, laced with lavender, lure her into a deep and soothing sleep. In a dream, a quiet voice speaks to her. It is the voice of someone who has travelled far and knows pain and suffering, faith and restoration. "Take courage, my child. Listen to me, heed me and let me help you," says the voice. "You must believe in yourself as well as my promises. I have a journey for you and, though it may be long and winding, you will be light of step because you can lean on me when you grow weary. Have faith that I will take you on a personal journey to find Love and Freedom".

Chapter 5: **Fear**

It is the springtime and though the world is waking up, Hope feels that she has no place in it. From her upstairs window, she sees the snow has melted. Brave snowdrops poke their heads above the dark canopy of soil, bringing optimism to endless dark, dreary, empty days. She feels she will never amount to anything. She has been told that often. They said that to love oneself is akin to the sin of arrogance; that humility is a virtue. Feeling unloved, day after day, she hides in her attic room, wishing that someone might discover her and set her free.

Behind her heavy cloak, Hope's mind imprisons her with dark thoughts and strange imaginings. It fills her very being with an impenetrable veil of sadness. If only someone could tell her who she really is; an undiscovered heroine whose gentleness, humility and creative mind the world needs.

Chapter 6: **Trust**

Hope goes to bed, feeling sad and empty, pulling her thick blankets close to her. She looks forward to a deep, dreamless sleep and respite from troubled thoughts. In her dreams, a calm voice speaks clearly to her. She wonders if she is still awake or dreaming. She feels suspended between a half-asleep and wide-awake place, a strange and foreign land where no-one can reach her.

"Look in the mirror," the alluring voice says. "You are a wonderful creation. You are meant to be here. You are special and have a unique and important place in the world. Let's go and find it, together. Trust in my guidance and what I am telling you. Look in the mirror again when you wake up. Repeat my words to your reflection. Then you will start to believe they are true and that you have a purpose."

Chapter 7: **Wisdom**

Hope steps out from her attic room to find cotton wool clouds suspended in a luminous azure sky. The air is crisp and fragrant, and she feels she has swallowed a cool pure glass of life itself. She sees a carpet of snowdrops; tiny bells on slender stems. They remind her how fragile she feels, hanging her head in shame. "I am not meant to be here," she tells herself. "I must go back inside. I am completely alone and suspended over a great huge void which is going to swallow me up so I will never be seen or heard of again".

Suddenly she realises she is not alone. A man is standing by the trees, wearing a beautiful white cloak. He speaks to her with the wisdom of the ages. She recognises it as the voice in the dream. "Hey, what's wrong?" he asks. She immediately feels at ease. "Everything and nothing," says Hope. "I have a destination but have no idea how to get there". "What is your name?" the stranger asks. "Hope" she whispers. "Then Hope is your destination and I will guide you there," the man says. "All that you are going through you must write down. For one day you will reach your destination and make a fresh new start. There you will meet those who feel lost and betrayed and help them to find their place of hope and new beginnings; that sense of being they are seeking. But you will need something for your journey".

He hands her a brown paper parcel tied up with a length of string. "Take this and put it on. It will equip you for all that lies ahead, on your new journey". As quickly as he appears, he is gone, leaving Hope alone with her thoughts.

Chapter 8: **Confidence**

ope's thoughts are heavy tonight, like her cloak. She feels guilty, as though she has been living a lie all these years. Named Hope, she has let hope die. She does not know what to do about it. Somehow, she feels the answer to her dilemma lies inside the package. In the confines of her attic room, she pulls on the string and out falls a white cloak, light as gossamer and soft as silk. It is beautiful, with an ethereal quality like the wise stranger.

Hope takes off her heavy black cloak and puts on the new one. It feels cool and warm at the same time. A piece of paper falls out of the pocket. On it are written the words, "Wear this cloak. It will keep you safe on the next important part of your journey to find Freedom. Be brave and never give up on Hope. Have the courage to start again and leave the past behind. You won't feel lonely anymore, but confident in who you are meant to be. You will no longer feel guilty and ashamed".

Chapter 9: **Anticipation**

Every day, Hope wakes with a feeling of growing anticipation and optimism. She wants to meet the stranger who has given her the white silk cloak. Although she does not know him, she trusts him and wants to ask his advice. She feels he has the answer to what she is seeking. He too has lost his way and been trapped in disappointment, like a beautiful butterfly caught in a spider's web, cocooned tightly so he could not spread his wings. He has suffered greatly but has endured on his quest to find Freedom. He can show her how to do the same.

Talking to him makes her burden of problems seem lighter and easier to bear. Each day she puts on her new cloak and ventures further and further into the woods to seek him out. Wearing the cloak, she no longer feels vulnerable and in danger, although she still feels lonely and disconnected. But when she takes off her cloak, she feels suffocated by a whirlpool of troubled thoughts which conscript her into a shallow, fitful sleep. She is left caught in a maze of blind alleys, with no way out of the life she is trapped within.

Chapter 10: **Courage**

Today Hope wakes up with a headful of cotton wool thoughts and no clarity. She knows she has somehow taken the wrong turning in life. It has led her nowhere and she will have to start over again. But her oasis of courage is dry and she has nothing to draw upon.

It had not always been so. She had once been a bright, social butterfly, her life a rich kaleidoscope of colour, new encounters and experiences. None of this seems real any more. She feels drained and desolate. Someone has stamped on her dreams and stolen her trust, making her feel isolated and afraid.

Tired and listless due to lack of rest, Hope drags herself out of the darkness to peep out of her casement window at the day's dawn. She goes through the motions of washing, dressing and combing her long blonde hair. She puts on her cloak and ventures out into the promise of a perfect blue spring day, unfolding its wings to the golden sun. Her thoughts are like waves crashing to the shore, only to rise up and buffet her once more. Sad and broken like her dreams, Hope knows that she must hold fast to courage, start over and find a new direction.

Chapter 11: **Perseverance**

Unlike other days, Hope walks on and on through the woods until her feet ache. As she does, her dark mood lightens. She reaches a babbling brook whose tinkling notes soothe her troubled thoughts. She dangles her sore feet in the cool water and lies down on the grassy bank, a velvet pillow beneath her tired head.

When she wakes up the stranger is there. His clear blue, iridescent eyes seem to know everything about her. She feels she could almost drown in them and that he knows the reason why she took the wrong path and how she can find a different one to Redemption and Freedom.

"I have been watching you as you sleep and see how beautiful you are to the core of your being. But you have lost your way and are hurting and I want to help you," he says.

He takes her hand and helps her up, then brings her back home to her attic room. "But why are you taking me back?" she asks. "I want to go forwards with you".

"Trust me," he says. "You must pace yourself and take some rest before the next and final stage of your journey".

Chapter 12: **Hope**

Back in her silent room, Hope hears chatter and laughter tinkling across the breeze like musical notes from a harpsichord. Throwing open her window, she looks out to see revellers in party outfits going towards the castle. They look happy and full of dreamy optimism, enjoying each other's company and looking forward to their evening plans. "How wonderful to be invited to the Great Hall at the castle," Hope says to herself. "Their banquets are renowned for being elite, exclusive, grand occasions. I would love to go but wouldn't know how to get invited and I don't have the right clothes to wear. I would never fit in".

She feels the need to pack a few belongings into a small case and lays out her clothes for tomorrow. Then she creeps into bed and cries herself to sleep. In her dreams the stranger comes to her, telling her she has nothing to fear and never to lose hope. She is going on a journey she has already begun, and the first step is always the hardest. All she must do now is continue on the next stage of her journey.

She sleeps soundly for the first time in years, feeling she is coming home and all will be well in the end.

Chapter 13: **Freedom**

Hope wakes early, writing in her diary one last time before the night melts into morning. Flicking through the earlier pages, she sees how she often felt like a fly caught in a sticky web. The more she struggles to get free, the more trapped she becomes, held captive against her will. She writes on a new page, "I am Hope and today I am going to find Freedom". She wonders if yesterday was a dream. Had she really met the wise stranger?

As Hope opens the door and steps out, she notices that the light is golden, the air is balmy and it feels like the first day of summer. Her thoughts are calm because she feels rested. She goes into the woods and sees the stranger waiting by a tree. He takes her belongings and sends them ahead, she's not sure where. But she trusts they will arrive at the destination to which she is heading. They walk a long way, making excellent progress, arriving at a babbling brook similar to the one she had found before. Close by, there are a group of people, each painting a beautiful picture. They are the partying revellers from the previous evening. But something is missing. She walks up to them and asks them what they are doing.

"We are painting the gurgling brook, the blue sky and the golden sun but we need a subject. Would you like to sit for us and let us paint you?" they said. "I don't feel important enough," she says. "Yes, you are," they say. "Let us paint what we see. Then you will know who you are."

Chapter 14: **Redemption**

Hope looks at the finished painting and sees that each one has captured a different essence of her character. One has captured courage, another sweet gentleness, a third trust, a fourth self-awareness, a fifth peace and a sixth hopefulness. "This is you," they say. "This is your picture of Hope". They have put her in the picture. Now she can see who she really is. She feels a part of life again.

They begin to pack up their easels. "Where are you going?" she asks. "The castle," they say. "We have been invited there tonight. Do you want to come along?"

"Yes," she says. "But I have nothing to wear". They take their paintbrushes and colours and paint her white cloak the colour of a summer's day; blue and gold and rose and lavender. When she puts it on, she feels she is a beautiful butterfly once more, flying free from earthly cares. "Please teach me to paint like you," she says. "Yes," they say. "We will".

The stranger has gone but in his place is Hope. He has given her the courage to start again, with friends to help her on her journey. To write her own story, for this is her story.

This is the Story of Hope and how she finds the courage to start out on a journey from Despair to Freedom.

Epilogue

I am Hope and though it took me a while to find my destination, I kept looking. In the end, I found the courage to start again and, on the way, I found myself. I came out of my Despair and I found Freedom.

This is what I have learned on my journey.

1. **Loneliness.** Everyone feels lonely in the dark times. But use those times to explore what you really want. And never stop dreaming. Your dreams are more real than life itself.
2. **Despair.** Don't give up. Everyone has a second chance of the life they were born to live.
3. **Doubt.** Don't sit indoors, worrying alone. If you do that, your fears might deceive you. There is a future and a hope for you out there.
4. **Faith.** Sleep well. Believe that in unlikely places, such as your dreams, you will find the answer you are seeking.
5. **Fear.** Don't give in to fear. Look for someone to encourage and motivate you. You cannot do this journey alone.
6. **Trust.** Look in the mirror and see who you really are, reflected in the eyes of those who love you. Trust those people.
7. **Wisdom.** Take wise counsel. You will find it if you look and listen hard enough, even though it might not be shouting at you.
8. **Confidence.** Exchange your dark cloak of despair for one of lightness and confidence. It will protect you from fear and keep you focused.
9. **Anticipation.** Open the door to the green shoots of new beginnings waiting to blossom into future opportunities.
10. **Courage.** Venture further and further out of your comfort zone. You will find inner strength by doing that.

11. **Perseverance.** Despite setbacks, don't think about going backwards, only forwards. Progress is the stepping stone to your true calling and final destination.

12. **Hope.** Prepare ahead. In those harsh, cold, dark, early days, believe that one day the sun will rise on a new life, the one you were born to live.

13. **Freedom.** Find friends to support you on the way. They are your trusted companions who will sustain you on your journey.

14. **Redemption.** Let your old dreams die in order to find new ones. Write what you have learned in a book. Turn that book into a plan and make that plan your destination. This is your Story of Hope. It's written especially for you.